Cryptogram Puzzle

In a cryptogram puzzle a phrase or quote

has its letters substitued with other letters.

For example, every "a" might be a "t",

every "e" might be a "w", and so on,

The letter substitution is consistent through the phrase.

For example, every "e" would be a "w" - throughout.

Key To The Solution

1: I=O   2: D=O   3: P=E   4: X=E   5: K=O   6: S=E   7: Z=O   8: U=O   9: F=O

10: A=I   11: C=I   12: T=I   13: S=E   14: B=I   15: T=O   16: S=O   17: I=E   18: B=O

19: W=O   20: V=T   21: C=T   22: K=I   23: D=E   24: P=A   25: N=O   26: T=O   27: W=T

28: X=T   29: J=I   30: S=I   31: Y=E   32: N=O   33: A=O   34: Q=O   35: I=E   36: M=I

37: J=I   38: F=N   39: M=N   40: B=E   41: G=T   42: F=T   43: N=T   44: L=T   45: Y=O

46: S=O   47: R=T   48: Z=O   49: Y=E   50: S=O   51: T=A   52: F=E   53: J=E   54: T=E

55: P=O   56: U=E   57: C=A   58: B=O   59: T=O   60: O=T

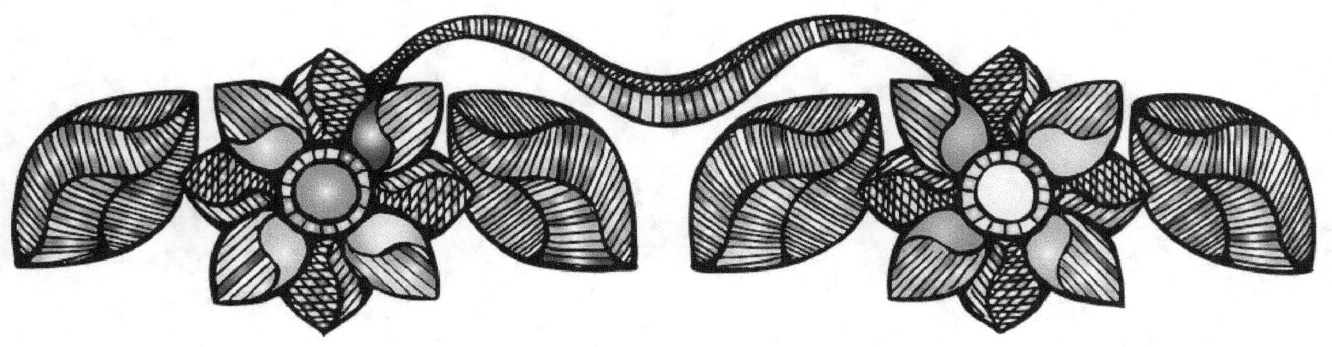

1) NIG ZWU YZWP IV HU, UDUWN YRUAU IV HU TIDUE NIG LZLN.

....

2) FDA RXNY RY ERBSY HDL PD LYXEDP, B GBSS PYMYL SYXMY FDA.

B GBSS SDMY FDA HDLYMYL.

....

3) XYCS MYOKP OH VOFP U HRPPQ HYTN QY JX LPUSQ.

O VYMP XYC.O WCHQ RUTQ QY VYMP XYC, UJ TYQ QYY ICHQ ZYS XYC HRPPQLPUSQ.

XYC USP VOFP GSPKOYCH WPRPV.

....

....

4) EYWR BWGX IFA RWUX CF QFTH, L YWDX NXXT EWLRLTH VFS RYLC GWI WQQ BI QLVX.

....

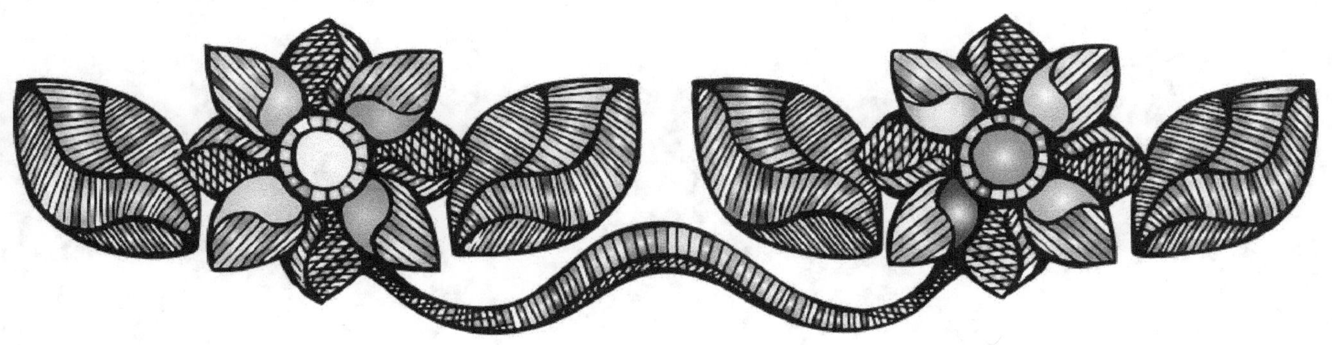

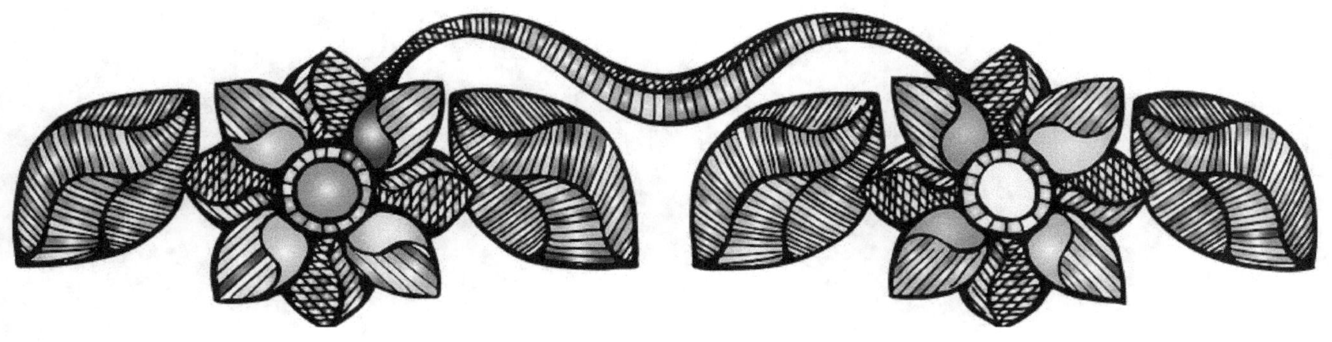

5) SO GKM SIDBUT SAI JRSAE FKI VKU JRT LKAITUVMH JRBAFO RSO DSIT, UTDTDZTU GKMUT KAT KV JRTD. XRTUBORTI SAI HKCTI. GKM SUT ONTXBSH JK DT. B HKCT GKM.

....

....

6) IL WNXS QNA LNY KD JYAS; K WNXS LNY PNR CPT QNASXSA.

....

7) ZBK BTMLF, T JTRLKP ZB Y RFYQ, JTRLKP FZ LYUK Y HQTKBP FZ SZUK HZQ STHK. CZBFLR IYRRKP, FLKB GYCK WKYQR. T RFYQFKP FZ SZRK LZIK YBP HTBYSSW T CKF LKQ. FLYF IKQRZB T JTRLKP HZQ TR WZX. T SZUK WZX.

....

....

8) AUP GYN G EYNZQUPJ MQDB BU SN, Q RNGYHA HUTN AUP.

Q BYPHA HUTN GKR BYNGJPYN AUP.

....

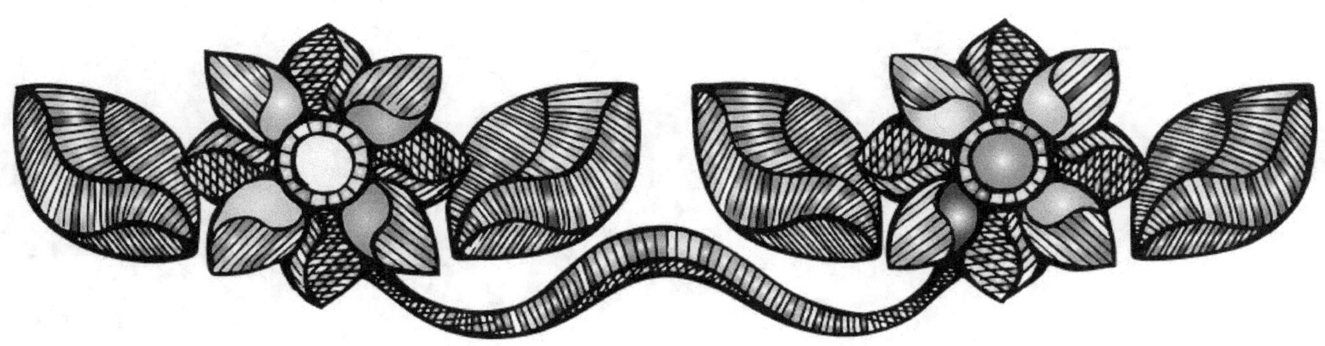

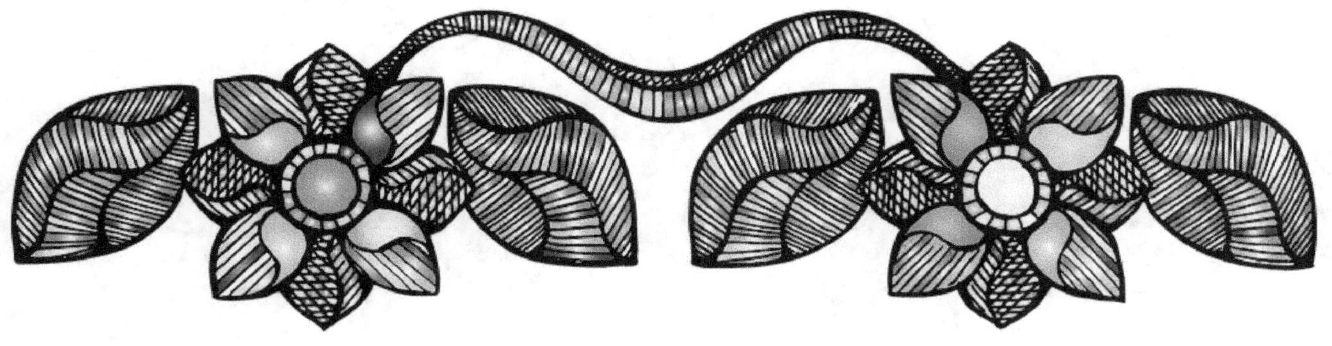

9) NPQVMKA, OFL PQT RF RWTHMPV JF UT, M XMVV VFCT OFL TCTQO RTHFKN FY UO VMYT.

....

....

10) FNR GPO GMM AK KOOT AK ULAE WNRPKOF; A BAMM VO BAUL FNR RKUAM ULO OKT.

....

....

11) IWL C LCZI C LSZ YAWZP DW JWN VCXID EWL, C LWNAG XCMP JWN S LSVK, ZLPPD INX SEG UCZZ. C AWMP JWN.

....

....

12) CYZH T RO CTLY QUK, T IZZW WTEZ T RO TH YZRPZH.

....

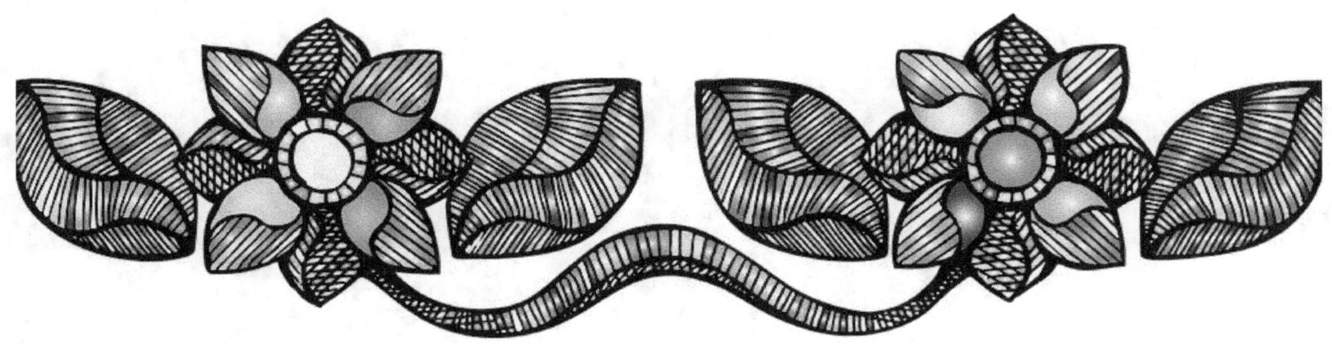

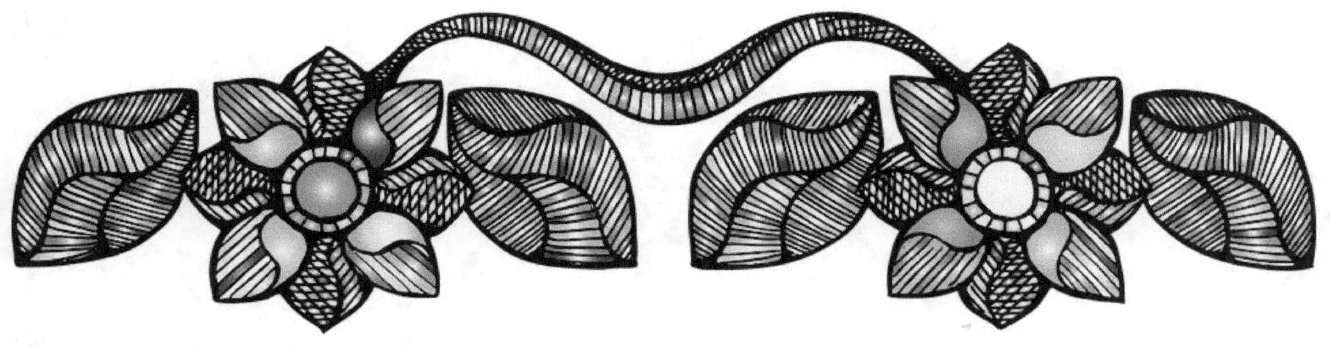

13) CMSKS EZ OD ZEOQUS FNP E IEUU ZCDW UDTEOQ PDY, PDY NKS AP FNEUP HKSNF.

....

14) B DBQQ ZWS TCTWS NTRW DKTY SIA HWS.DKTY QBPT BV ZBPPBHAQN, B DBQQ RQDRSV XT
NKTWT PIW SIA.

....

....

15) KTE RSX PZX TFOK HXSBTF PZRP QRUXB QK OVDX QXRFVFYDEO. OTLX KTE.

....

16) GSF RXL ES XLIRXYRJWL; GSFX WSOL ARE PSPRWWG UARTMLH IG WVZL. V URTP JLWVLOL V
ILP ESILSTL RE BSTHLXZFW RE GSF. VZ V BRE PSWH V BSFWH LOLX ILLP GSF, V BSFWHTP
JLWVLOL. GSF RXL RT RIRKVTM WRHG. V WSOL GSF.

....

....

....

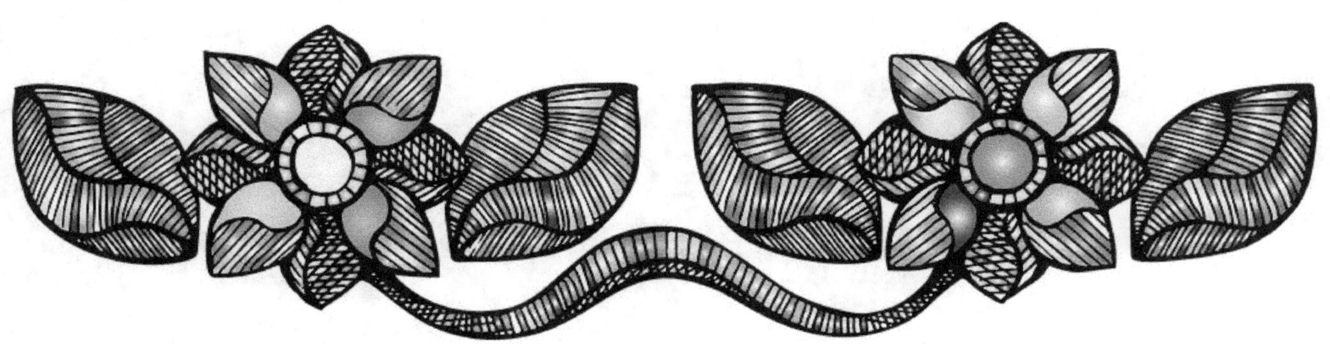

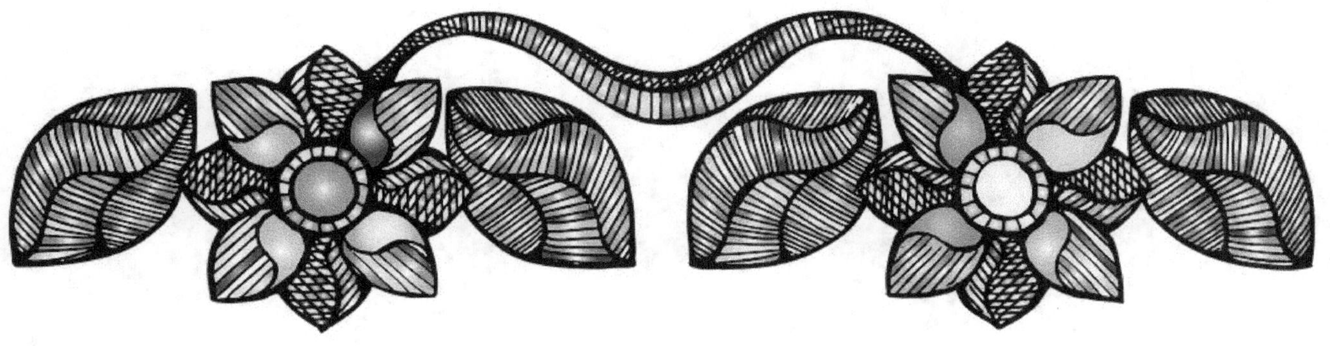

17) PS XIDTM DCKDSE SIDTAE YLT SLNT CLBI. R CLBI SLN FIDTCS.

....

18) T DPBX PBQJTPC YFMQM HBSGLGS, GLGSN METYG FPU YFACJQGS XG JFLG MJFSGU FPU
KBPQTPAG QB, RSBLGM QB EG QJFQ QJG EGEBSTGM BH BAS HSTGPUMJTR XTYY YFMQ HBS QJG
SGMQ BH EN YTHG.

....

....

....

19) AWH YSD EA DJDSAUVZCI YCP AWH EDYC UVD OWSBP UW ED. Z BWJD AWH.

....

20) NB IPYA, DN ZPHHB VP FDZVGHW BPG. XIVRPGSR, VRDZ DZ GHSACV. D QXCV BPG VP ZACF
NA BPGH UDJVGHA HDSRV CPQ. DN UIXBDCS JXHFZ QDVR NB KHDACFZ XCF D IPZV NB EGAAC.

....

....

....

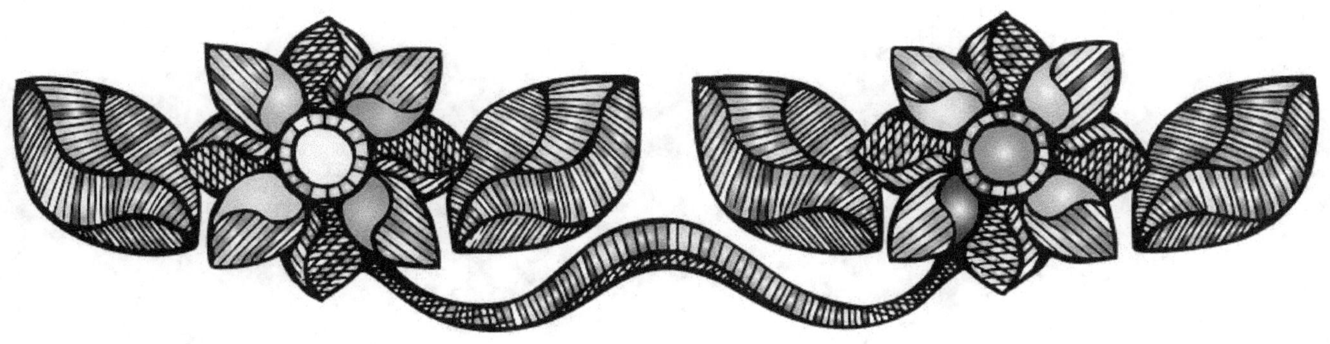

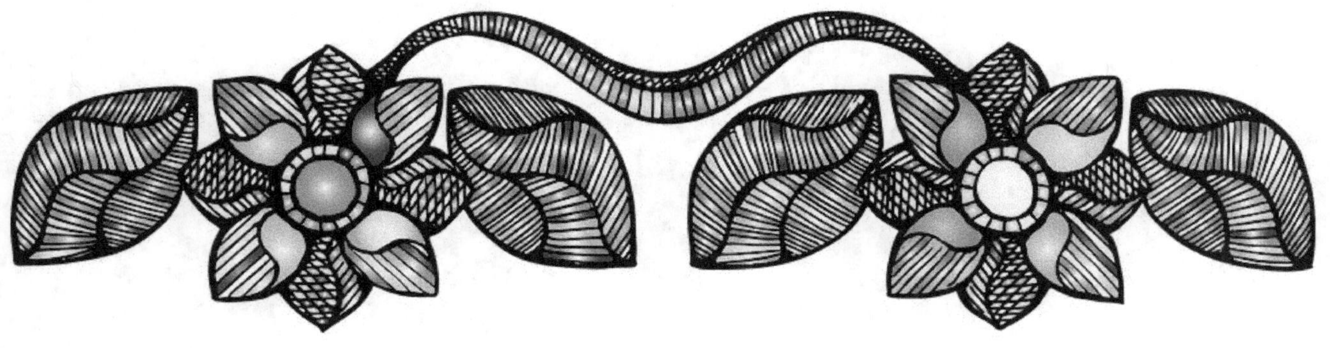

21) CLWBO VJS YJZ HLJJQDBK CJ CZWRAN JB CLDQ FWCL EDCL GA. D EDNN BARAZ NAC VJS PJEB, WQ VJS WZA GV FAZYAHC GWCHL

....

....

22) SZSW AMSW DMSCS KY WT YRWYMKWS KW GH VKJS, K YDKVV VTZS HTR.

....

23) BJIYA WCJVD SWVVJL DHOIDAA LKD YDOLK JP TN CJQD PJI NJM. TN WSLUJVA BUCC AODWR CJMYDI LKWV BJIYA. U CJQD NJM!

....

....

24) XZV POK NZSSKO SNPI PIXSNLIU LI SNLW RZOEQ; XZV HPFK HX NKPOS GKPS TPWSKO.

....

....

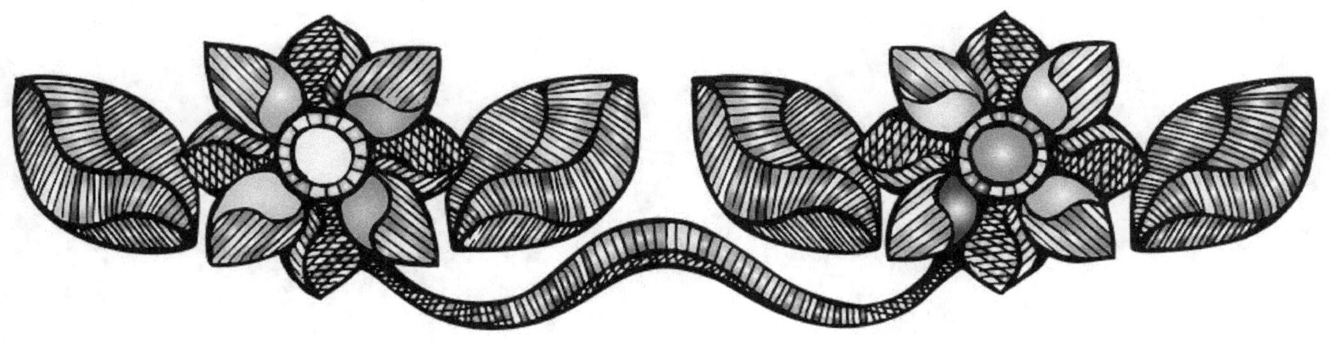

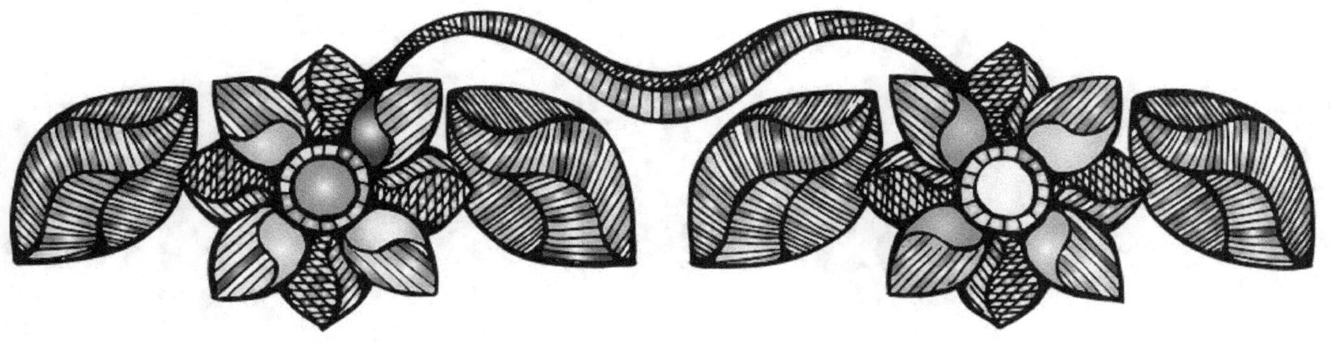

25) FNR YOX AUX VXF AN GF UXYOA.T YG 100% TQ CNHX JTAU FNR.

....

26) PTLA NTDS CW FTV TFS TU VKS VKCFMW C FSSE VT UXYS NCUS YKXNNSFMSW.

 C NTDS PTL ZXZP.

....

....

27) K UOCJ SJJF CJVX EMGIX WUVYMBU HX JFWKVJ EKPJ. WJEE HJ KP WUKZ KZ FYW WVMJ. K
UOCJ UOL YFJ YP WUJ SJZW JLMGOWKYF, WUJ SJZW PVKJFLZ, SJZW JLMGOWKYF OFL FYN UJVJ
XYM OVJ, WUJ SJZW EYCJV KF WUJ NYVEL.

....

....

....

28) CBO XWY DZQNUY XB AC WREEQLYHH, Q IRLX QARUQLY MQPQLU SQXWBOX CBO.

....

....

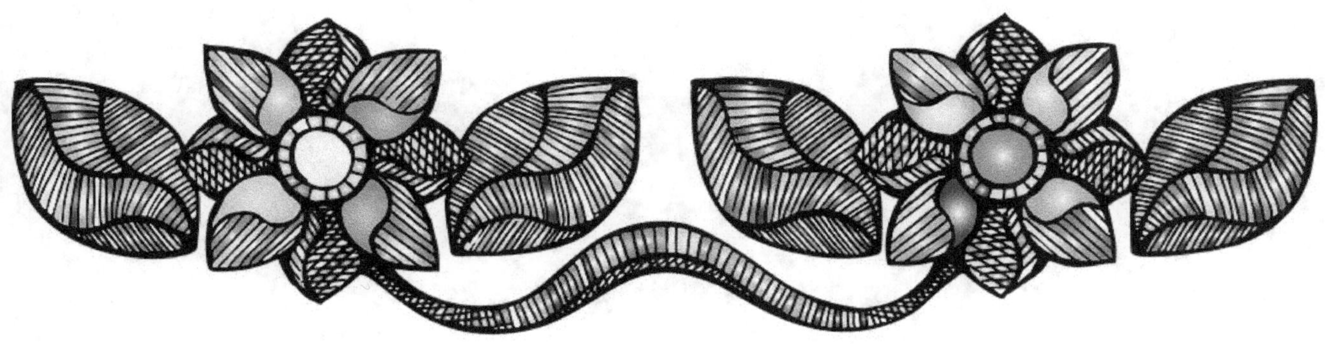

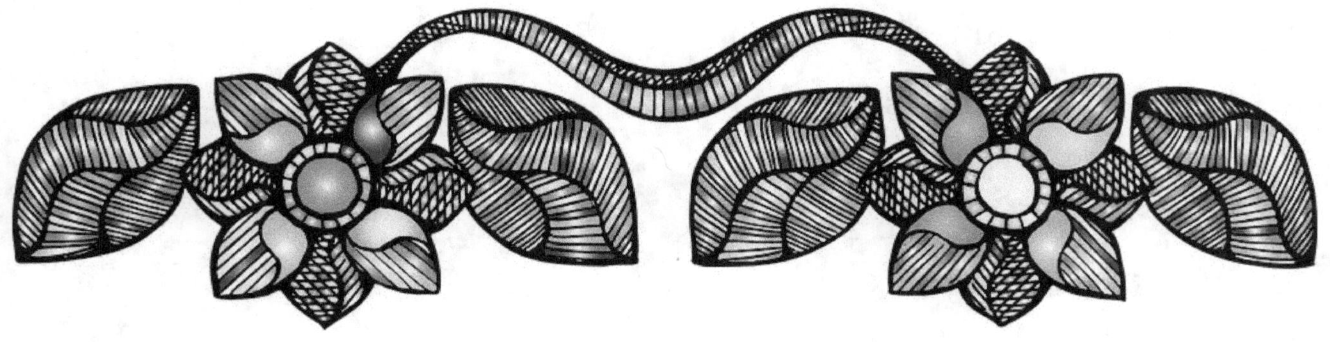

29) ITISH YJRI J OCCN JDYC HCVS IHIF, J AGDY EIOJITI MCX EIGVYJBVO HCV GSI.

....

30) RKRIVEOSGD S AJ, MRHAF EJ VJN. S DSKR VJN WV MSLR.

....

31) CXQ THY EC IXUTC TVU BXHYKYH. JXKY CXQ.

....

32) W JINXWHL UN GL VWUE QNB YNILPLI, ZN XOUULI ENV XOZQ DEOTTLZKLH W VWTT YODL.

....

....

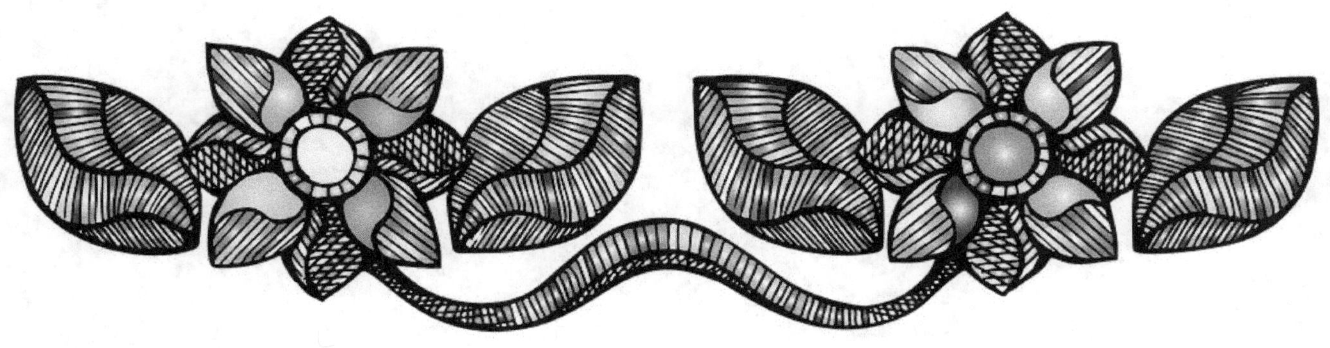

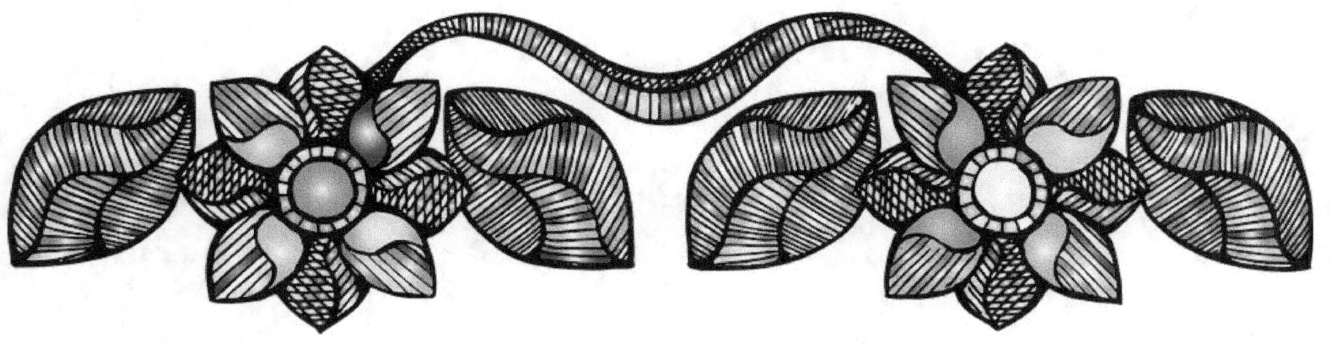

33) VDQZBJY, LH NFDQR KFDRM OAQ HAT; HAT OBZZ LH ZBOF CBRN PAH. B DL MA YQDRFOTZ RA NDWF HAT BJ LH ZBOF.

....

....

34) WQS JGR CNR AQSGOR QT KW IQW. Y ZYAN CNYA CRHPA CQ RCRGHYCW. Y EQXR WQS.

....

....

35) BU QARBGH TAE BP O ZYBNI, KFIG B JAEQV QARI KA ZANNBK KFI ZYBNI XIZOEPI QBUI JBKFAEK TAE BP NIOGBGHQIPP.

....

....

36) MD OSRK FSD YGDDRT PSJ VSFZ M JGMD, M JMVV KDMVV JGMD AST USX, AST USX GTR DPR OTRGY SF YU VMAR.

....

....

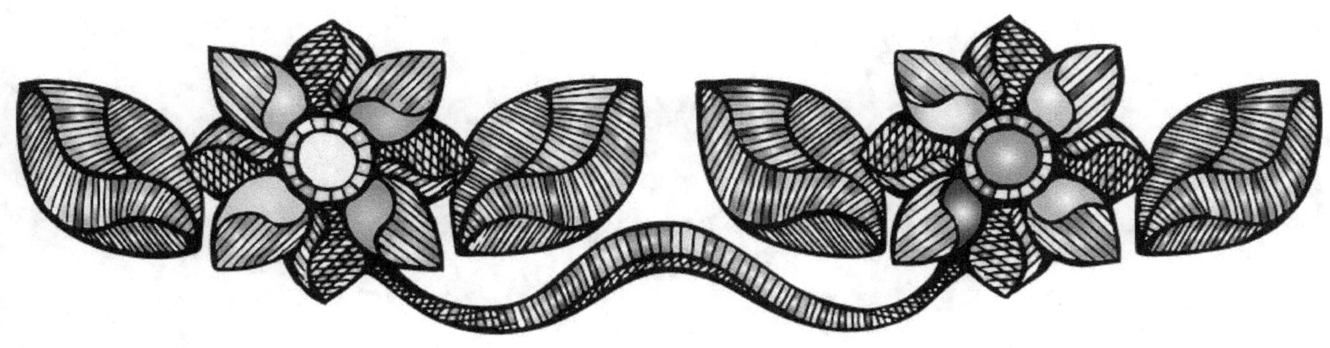

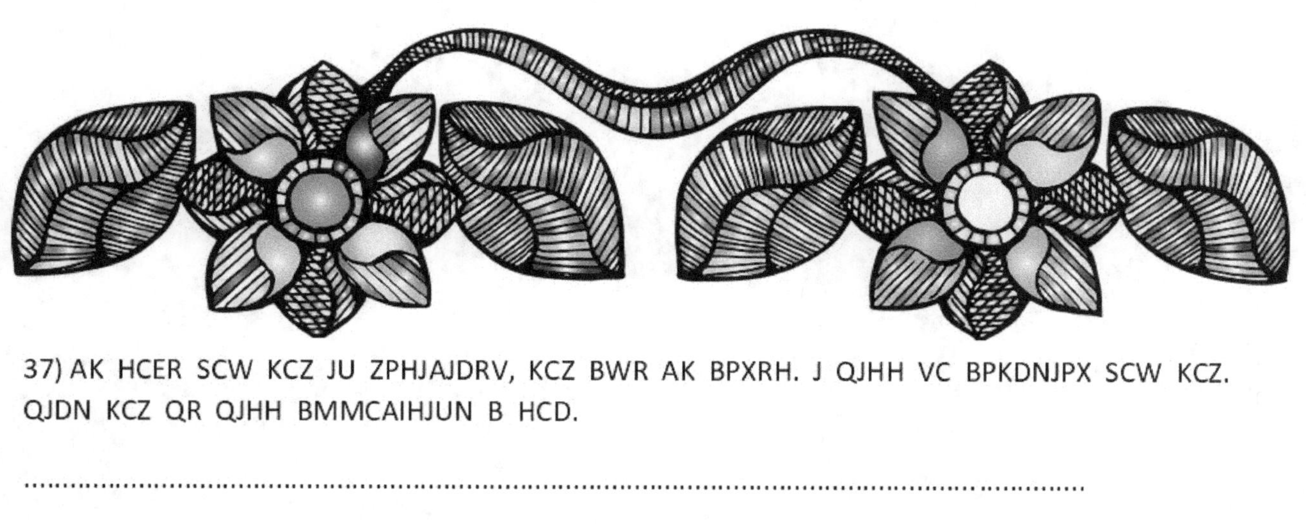

37) AK HCER SCW KCZ JU ZPHJAJDRV, KCZ BWR AK BPXRH. J QJHH VC BPKDNJPX SCW KCZ. QJDN KCZ QR QJHH BMMCAIHJUN B HCD.

....

....

38) JGFVAULQBULEGFO WGA ZEFFEFV UF UZUAP GW TREFV LNR CGOL TRUQLEWQB VEAB EF LNR ZGABP. LNR VAUFP YAEJR EO CM BGDR WGA MGQ.

....

....

39) GHGNV FZNMKMQ, DYG OGSXDKJXI NKBKMQ BXM FSPGB FG YSAAV SML KM DYG GHGMKMQ, DYG BXMLZRMGN SML WZZIKMQ ONGGEG ONKMQB S BFKIG ZM FV JSWG. DYG WYKNAKMQ OKNLB ONKMQ TZV DZ FV YGSND. SII DYKB KB MZD WZFAIGDG XMDKI K BGG VZXN IZHGIV

....

....

....

40) IHL XPB YI XZTBW.

....

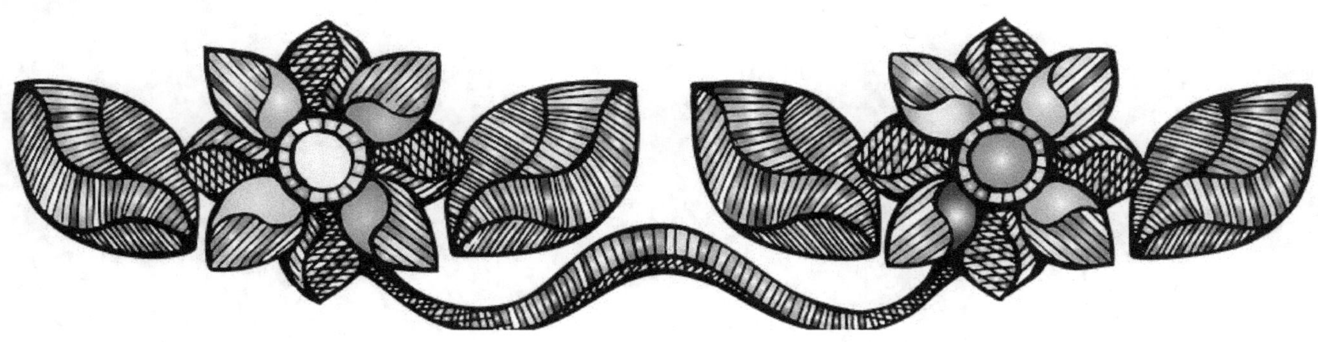

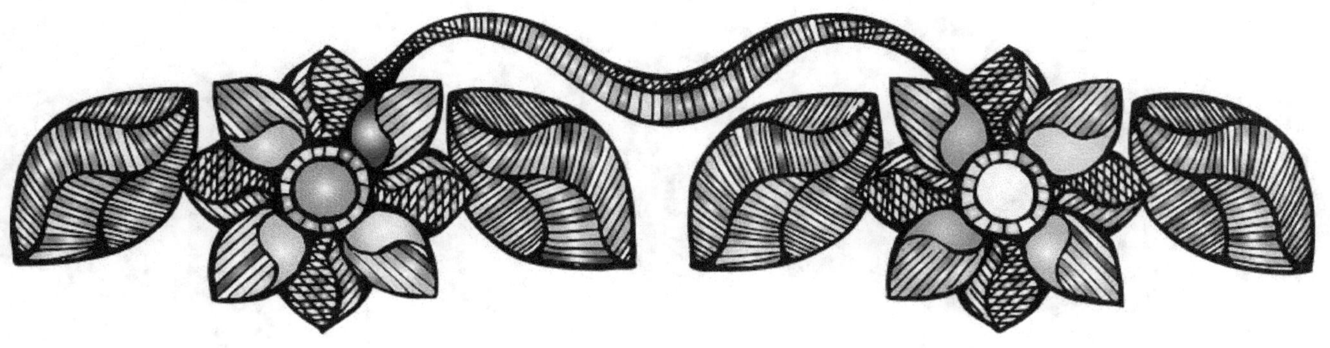

41) XAZ DQB GUB JBVG GUHEI GUDG UDV BWBQ UDKKBEBN GA LB. H SHFF DFSDXV YHIUG YAQ XAZ DEN JB GUBQB YAQ XAZ.

....

....

42) SLIQ O GZ SRJJOIT, O NIF HR CIGERDH.OFH RQEW FLGF O ERMI WRD GQT O TRQF SGQF FR ERHI WRD.

....

....

43) NYU CXRFSDRUZ NSFEI DEC PUZI GUEXNJWXQ GXN JN DEC RSN EC GUEXNJWXQ EC ISX LI QSPU.

....

....

44) LAZPZ CJ JDSZLACXV SNVCFNR NODHL BDH, BDHP JSCRZ, NXY BDHP ZBZJ, JD OZNHLCGHR. XD SNLLZP TANL C NS NRTNBJ NLLPNFLZY LD BDH.

....

....

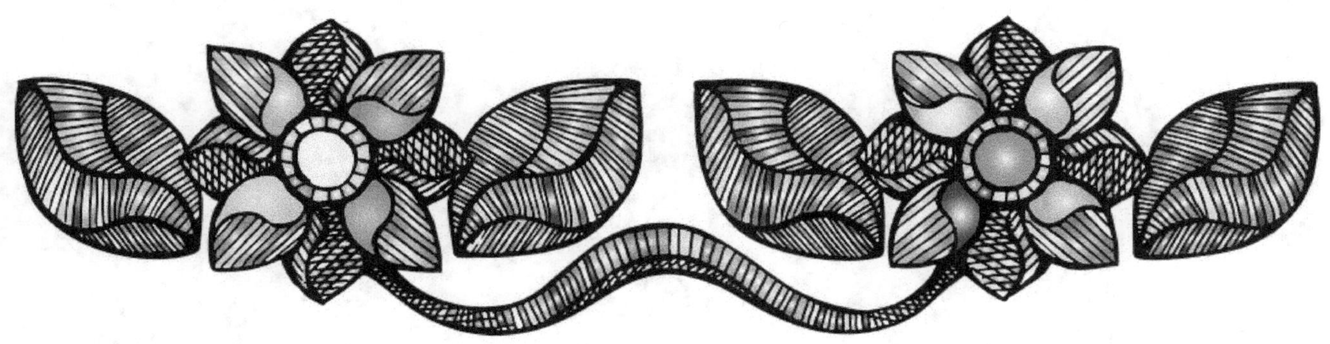

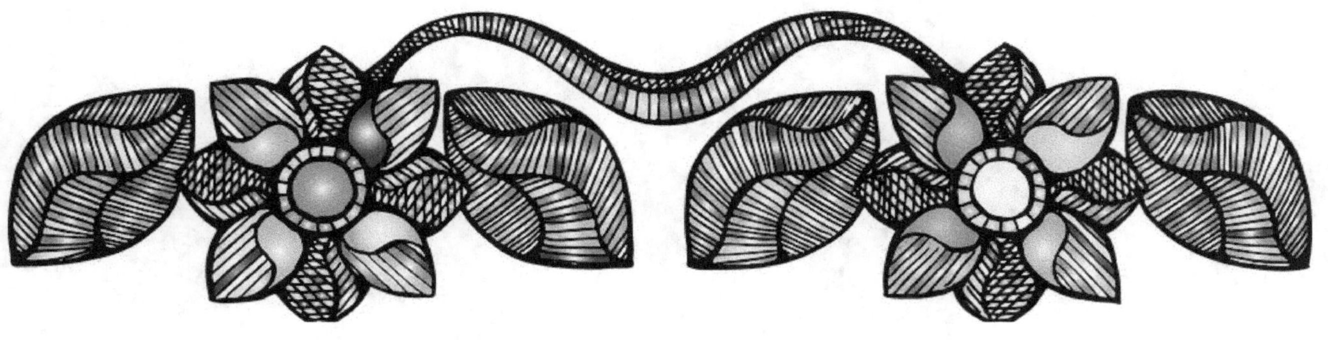

45) T ES RY IFGTZIA ZY RUEQI ZUTR VYWI CTZU NYX, NYX EQI SN IWIQNZUTPJ EPA T VYWI NYX AIEQVN.

....

....

46) GQ BYDY OS QKVY MSP BKUUM, G UDSQGJY OS XYAYD NYO MSP RSTX SD OS QKVY MSP WDM, CYWKPJY MSP KDY OBY SXNM OBGXL GX NGZY OBKO QKOOYDJ OS QY.

....

....

47) RYJT JT XQ UHPC EHL QHV. J NBZR RH WJPC QHV RYC MCTR RYJZWT J KBZ BEEHLI, TGCZI RYC MCTR RJXC J KBZ TGBLC NJRY QHV, TYBLC XQ RLCBTVLCI UJEC XHXCZRT NJRY QHV, BUU NJRY ZH LCRVLZ COGCKRBRJHZT.

....

....

....

48) GOFJBYD, YZ ZYL XOK LELF KVZJLY UN XLOFV, JBRL NZC XOEL GZYL. B XOEL GLHBGL VZ QL TBVX NZC OJJ UN JBPL.

....

....

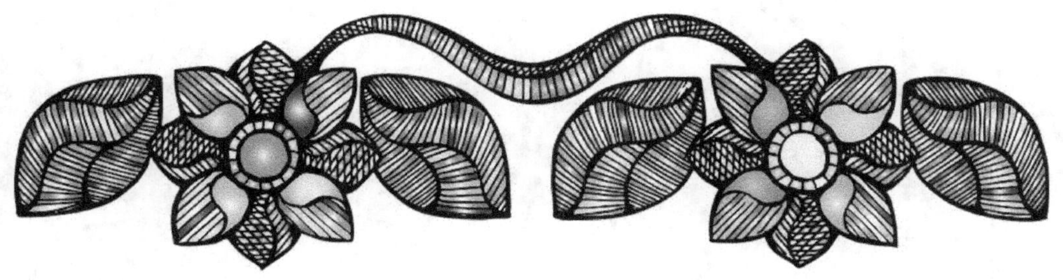

49) MNZQ ZQ P OYPSZMI. QEDYEWY BNE SEFYQ PWH PHEOYQ IEC BZSS WEM EWSI MYSS IEC NEB MNYI RYYS. MNYI BZSS JE ECM ER MNYZO BPI ME QNEB IEC NEB DCXN MNYI SEFY IEC. NELY IEC QYY MNY PXMZEWQ EW NEB DCXN Z SEFY IEC.

....

....

....

50) KSE JLC GAC TSUG VCJEGFHEN WCLUSQ F GAC ZASNC ZSLNY. F WLSTFUC GS NSMC JQY GLCJUELC KSE.

....

....

51) QBVO UBML ZW TW WBBDNZAX TW DNL WYOZAX, TW NZXN TW DNL WJQ, TW WFLLD TW T NBALQKBIG, TW XOTKZBVW TW DNL UZUZLW TAC TW OLTU TW QBV. Z UBML QBV IQ CLTO.

....

....

....

52) KSWDF XK SCF RCT SCGK QFRDE OFRE. Y GSIF KSW JS XWHQ.Y GSIF FIFDKEQYCN ROSWE KSW.

....

....

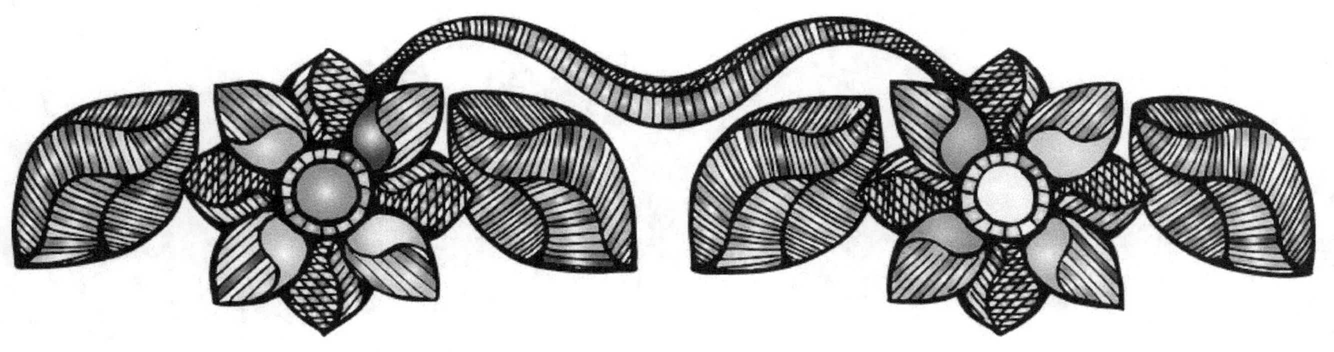

53) PTY FKJ QT MJFYDOVYW; PTY FWAFPQ XFCJ XJ FBXOKJ PTY.

....

54) W IF JIVVD QP XT DPHC EPGT.DPH ICT FD KIGPCWQT, QJT EPGT PK FD EWKT.

W EPGT DPH.

....

....

55) PYW PX V CUMMUPS FZPFMZ US WBZ GPHMN, U BVOZ DBPKZS PSML PSZ FZHKPS WP
MPOZ, DBZHUKB, FHPWZDW VSN VMGVLK CZ WBZHZ XPH BZH. U MPOZ LPY.

....

....

56) RN VMLU, H TWJE EUVV IOWE H IMGVB BM IHEOMGE NMG XN RN ZHBU, NMG WAU RN
WVV. EOU VMLU MP RN VHPU, H VMLU NMG BUWAVN.

....

....

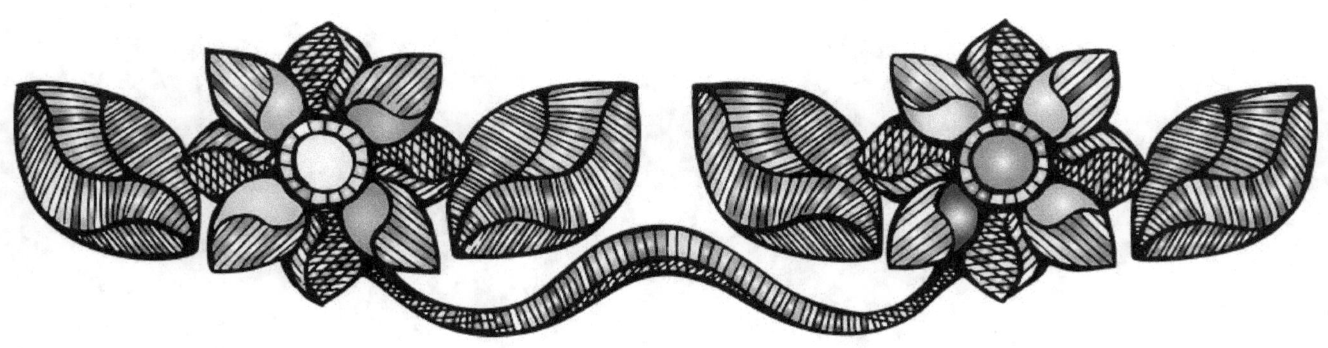

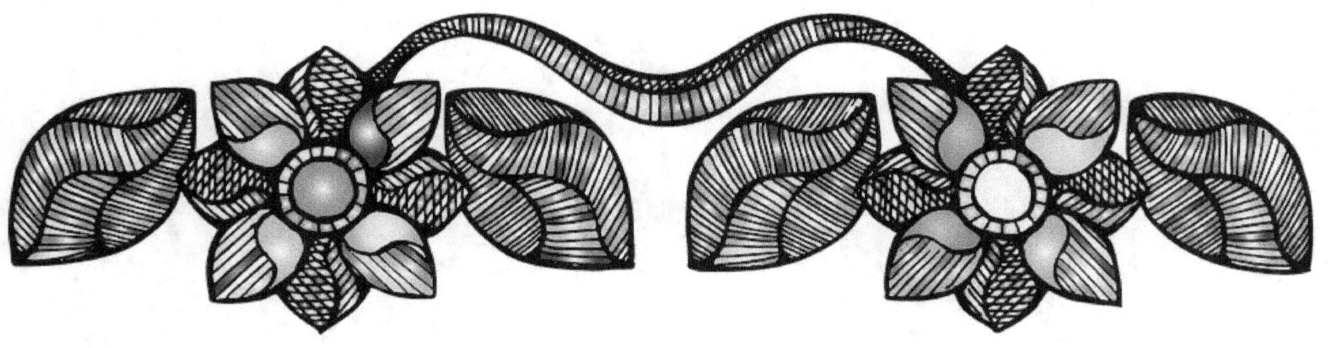

57) DCRH KH CL OTSX QXHCK KCP, CPQ B ZBYY KCRH OTSX QXHCKL FTKH DXSH. YTGH KH DAH
ZCO B CK, CPQ B ZBYY FAHXBLA OTS DAH ZCO OTS ZCPD HGHXO QCO.

....

....

58) GKPHU K IUD SBW, IS VKRU YLG MNULDVS HYLPMUC; IS VKRU YLG HYLPMUC RBN MBBC. IS
CNULIG YLOU MNBXP IBNU LPC IBNU. K MKOU IBNU, K VLWMY IBNU, K DYKPQ IBNU LPC RUUV
GB VBOUC EUHLWGU BR SBW IS VBOU.

....

....

....

59) A BAUQ VTW JV GAKQ; QUQNVEIAHB A TYH AC XGG VTWNC. ITMQ VTW YAGG HTE
ZACXMMTAHE JQ. A GTUQ VTW.

....

....

60) P NCVO THNPO OATO P FTDO UEC PD NU XPLY. P BTDO AEXH TDU XEDIYS.

....

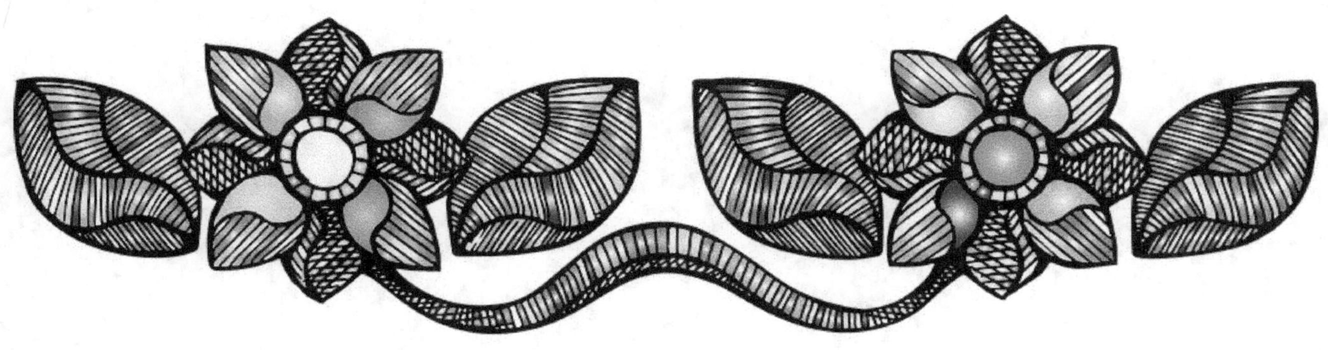

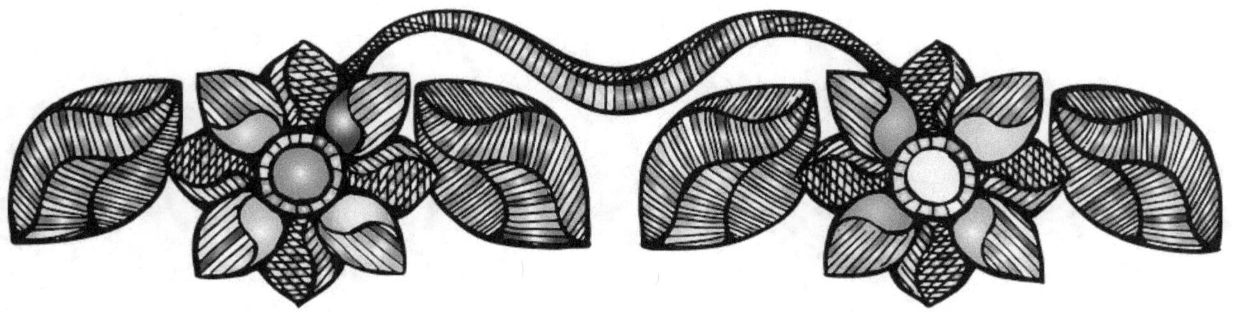

The Solved Cryptograms

1) You are part of me, every piece of me loves you baby.

2) You make me smile for no reason, I will never leave you. I will love you forever.

3) Your voice is like a sweet song to my heart. I love you.I just want to love you,

am not too bust for you sweetheart.You are like precious jewel.

4) What made you take so long, I have been waiting for this day all my life.

5) As you admire and thank God for the wonderful things has made, remember youre one of

them. Cherished and loved. You are special to me. I love you.

6) My love for you is pure; I love you now and forever.

7) One night, I wished on a star, wished to have a friend to love for life. Months passed,

then came years. I started to lose hope and finally I met her. That person I wished

for is you. I love you.

8) You are a precious gift to me, I dearly love you.I truly love and treasure you.

9) Darling, you are so special to me, I will love you every second of my life.

10) You are all in need in this journey; I will be with you until the end

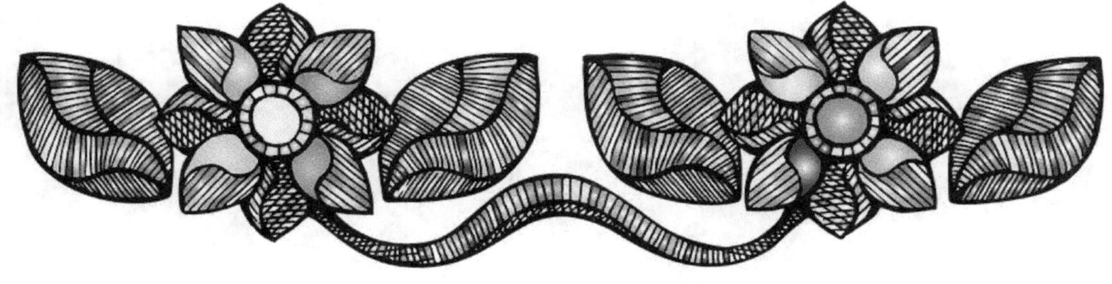

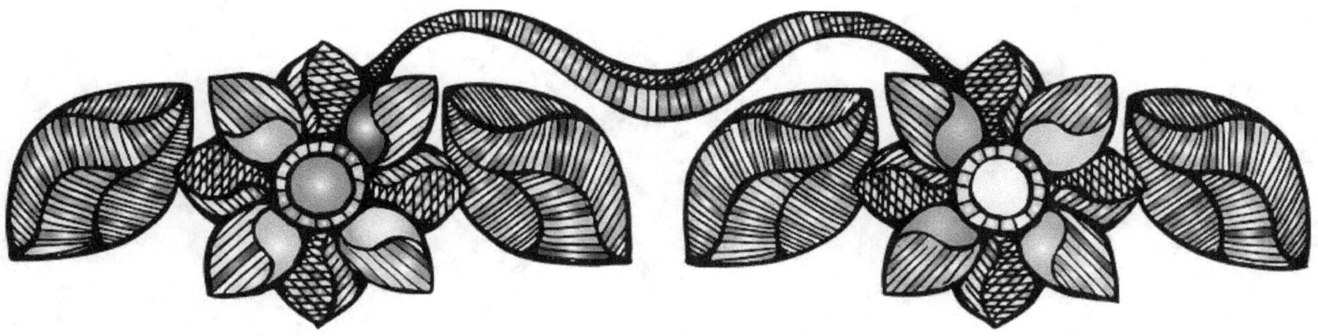

11) How i wish i was close to you right now, i would give you a warm, sweet hug and kiss. I

love you.

12) When I am with you, I feel like I am in heaven.

13) There is no single day I will stop loving you, you are my daily bread.

14) I will dry every tear when you cry.When life is difficult, I will always be there for you.

15) You are the only person that makes my life meaningful. Love you.

16) You are so remarkable; your love has totally changed my life. I cant believe I met someone as wonderful as you. If I was told I would ever meet you, I wouldnt believe. You are an amazing lady. I love you.

17) My heart always yearns for your love. I love you dearly.

18) I know nothing lasts forever, every smile and laughter we have shared and continue to,

proves to me that the memories of our friendship will last for the rest of my life.

19) You are my everything and you mean the world to me. I love you.

20) My love, Im sorry to disturb you. Although, this is urgent. I want you to send me your

picture right now. Im playing cards with my friends and I lost my queen.

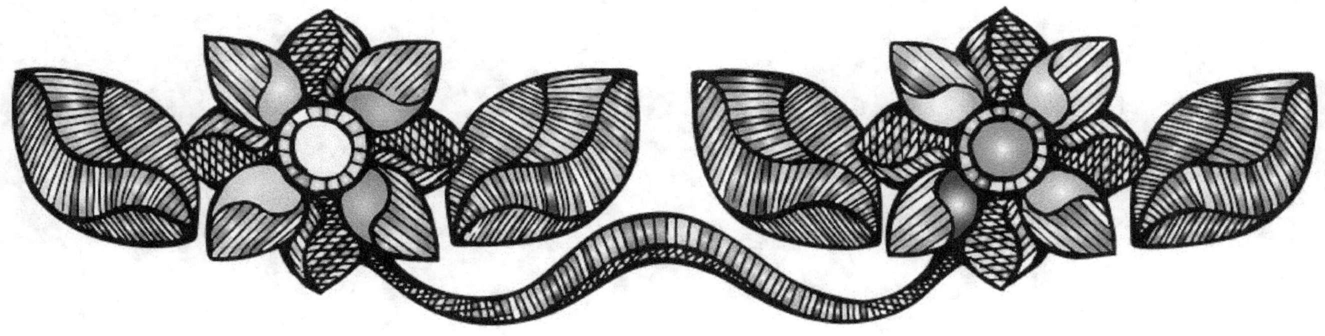

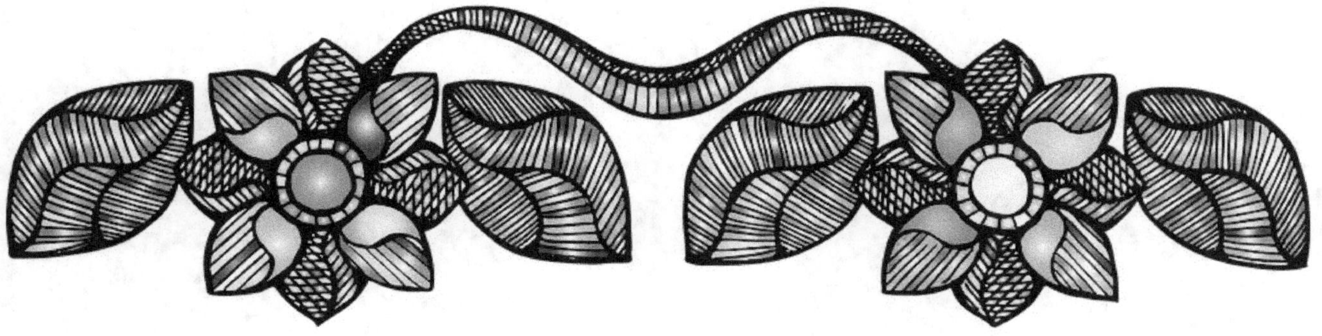

21) Thank you for choosing to travel on this path with me. I will never let you down, as you are my perfect match

22) Even when there is no sunshine in my life, I still love you.

23) Words alone cannot express the depth of my love for you. My actions will speak louder than words. I love you!

24) You are hotter than anything in this world; you make my heart beat faster.

25) You are the key to my heart.I am 100% in love with you.

26) Your love is not one of the things I need to face life challenges. I love you baby.

27) I have been very lucky through my entire life. Tell me if this is not true. I have had one of the best education, the best friends, best education and now here you are, the best lover in the world.

28) You the bridge to my happiness, I cant imagine living without you.

29) Every time I look into your eyes, I cant believe how beautiful you are.

30) Everything I do, leads to you. I give you my life.

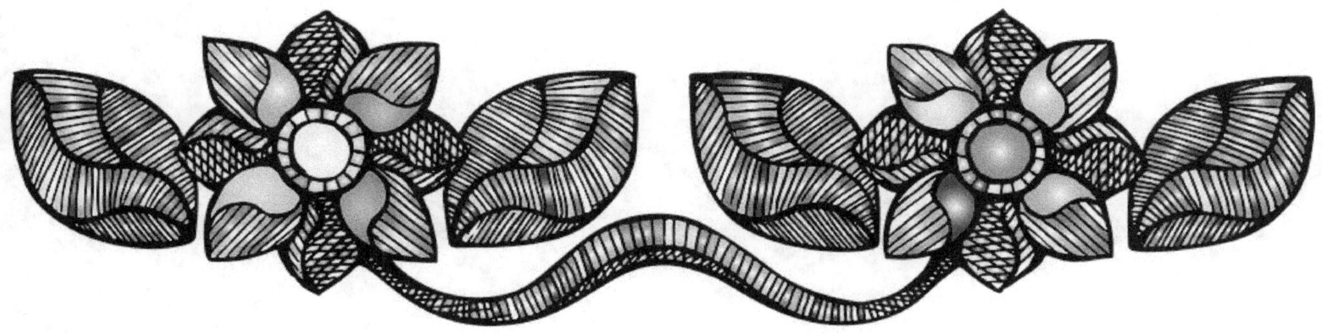

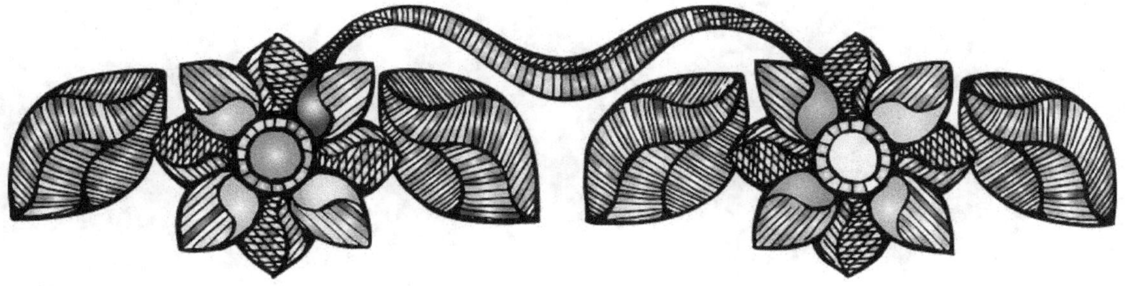

31) You are my today and forever. Love you.

32) I promise to be with you forever, no matter how many challenges I will face.

33) Darling, my heart beats for you; you fill my life with joy. I am so grateful to have you in

my life.

34) You are the source of my joy. I wish this tends to eternity. I love you.

35) If loving you is a crime, then I would love to commit the crime because life

without you is meaningless.

36) It does not matter how long I wait, I will still wait for you, for you are the dream on my

life.

37) My love for you is unlimited, you are my angel. I will do anything for you. With

you we will accomplish a lot.

38) Congratulations for winning an award of being the most beautiful girl in the

world. The Grand price is my love for you.

39) Every morning, the beautiful rising sun makes me happy and in the evening, the

sundowner and cooling breeze brings a smile on my face. The chirping birds bring

joy to my heart. All this is not complete until I see your lovely

40) You are my angel.

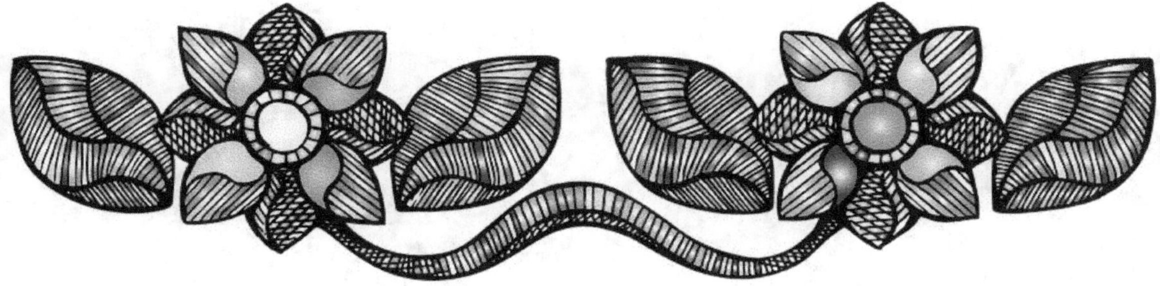

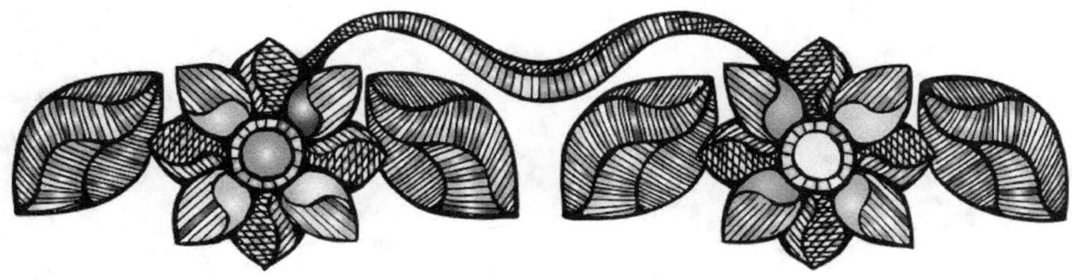

41) You are the best thing that has ever happened to me. I will always fight for you and be there for you.

42) When I am worried, I get so jealous.Its only that I love you and I dont want to lose you.

43) The sundowner today was very beautiful but it was not as beautiful as you my love.

44) There is something magical about you, your smile, and your eyes, so beautiful. No matter what I am always attracted to you.

45) I am so excited to share this love with you, you are my everything and I love you dearly.

46) Im here to make you happy, I promise to never let you down or to make you cry, because you are the only thing in life that matters to me.

47) This is my love for you. I want to give you the best things I can afford, spend the best time I can spare with you, share my treasured life moments with you, all with no return expectations.

48) Darling, no one has ever stolen my heart, like you have done. I have decide to be with you all my life.

49) This is a reality. Someone who loves and adores you will not only tell you how they feel. They will go out of their way to show you how much they love you. Hope you see the actions on how much I love you.

50) You are the most beautiful person I the whole world. I promise to love and treasure you.

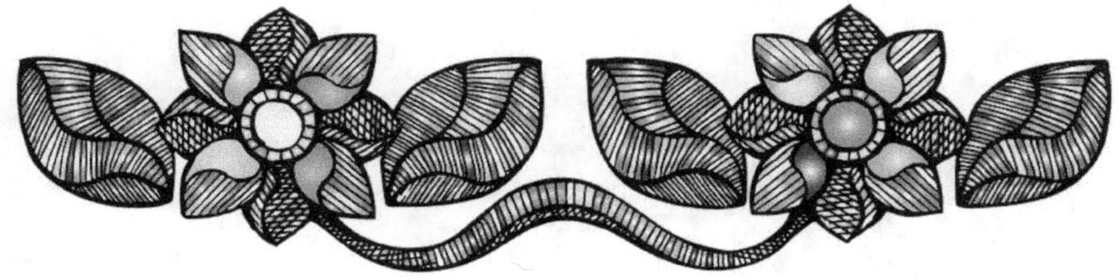

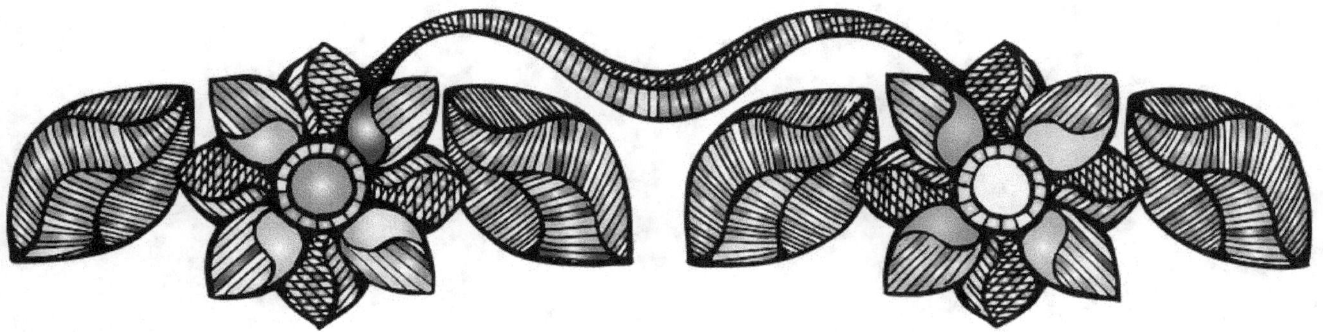

51) Your love is as soothing as the spring, as high as the sky, as sweet as a honeycomb, as gracious as the lilies and as real as YOU. I love you my dear.

52) Youre my one and only heart beat. I love you so much. I love everything about you.

53) You are so beautiful; you always make me admire you.

54) I am happy to be your love.You are my favorite, the love of my life. I love you.

55) Out of a billion people in the World, I have chosen only one person to love, cherish, protect and always be there for her. I love you.

56) My love, I cant tell what I would do without you by my side, you are my all. The love of my life, I love you dearly.

57) Take me as your dream man, and I will make your dreams come true. Love me the way I am, and I will cherish you the way you want every day.

58) Since I met you, my life has greatly changed; my life has changed for good. My dreams have grown more and more. I give More, I laugh More, I think more and feel so loved because of you my love.

59) I give you my life; everything I own is all yours. hope you will not disappoint me. I love you.

60) I must admit that I want you in my life. I cant hold any longer.

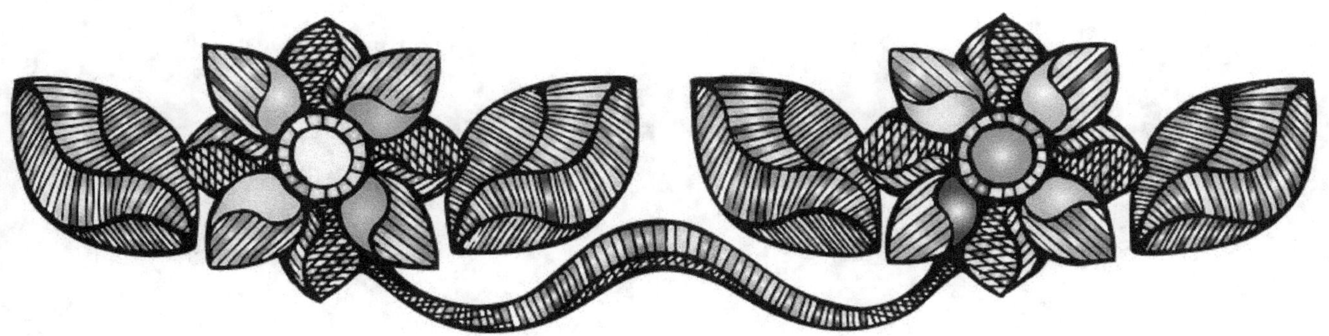

www.ingramcontent.com/pod-product-compliance
Lightning Source LLC
Chambersburg PA
CBHW080853160726
47999CB00009B/3106